A to Z of Becoming a Published Author Today

Don Allen Holbrook

ISBN:1493744496
ISBN-13:9781493744497

DEDICATION

I am writing this book because I feel everyone has a great story to tell. Far to often we allow others to dissuade us from following our passion. Being a published author is many folks dream. I wanted to help as many as possible make this dream come to a reality. There is nothing more fulfilling in my opinion that seeing others realize their dream of writing their first book and then getting it published so that they can pass along their own experiences to others in future generations.

CONTENTS

ACKNOWLEDGMENTS

Thank you to all my family and friends for your constant emotional support and friendship. I can't begin to name all of the people that have inspired me and guided me at different points of my life. But I am thankful for all of you. Your gifts of love, friendship, kindness and sometimes just listening have uplifted me so many times. I love you all.

THE MYTHS OF PUBLISHING
(SELF-PUBLISHING VERSUS TRADITIONAL)

CHAPTER 1

In order to become a published author, you need to actually write a book. Desiring to write a book and actually putting the effort into actually writing a book are two totally different things. Many people feel the urge to write a book or believe they have a wonderful story to tell, but putting forth the effort requires initiative. That is usually all that separates a successful author from a wannabe author. It is also why so many people hold authors with so much esteem. They recognize that the author has done something they themselves have for whatever reason not been able to accomplish. The process of writing a novel is an intensely personal one that, if it's going to be in any way rewarding, requires an intensely personal connection to the story you're trying to write. Don't be put off writing a manuscript and/or novel by the thought that the plot has to be mapped out with some secret complexity several months in advance and feature a vast cast of characters and/or very deep conceptual background. Most authors start writing without a clear idea of where they are going but a loose outline of what they want to cover and general specifics of what they know of each area. A writer looks for 'the extraordinary magic in the everyday experiences we all participate in and then makes such experiences come into a personal format that is compelling for their intended audience. Not everyone will love your work and that is perfectly fine. There are no finite rules for writing a great book, rather you should understand that stories are all around us and can be crafted by our own unique perspective or imagination of what if, to why. Perhaps the most important thing you have to bear in mind is what market you are writing for. To maximize your chances of success you need to write a book that can slot into an established genre, and where you have a good feel for the intended audience. It is for this reason alone there has been such a rash exponential growth of self-published independent authors. They are writing to a market and genre that they understand and sharing their own unique perspective with an audience of kindred spirits, in their lingo. The first choice is always is your work, fiction or Non-fiction? Fiction requires far more creativity but allows for far more flexibility of expression. Non-fiction requires a strong sense of factual nature and citing your sources or stating what is opinion versus fact very clearly. Both markets are also wildly different in size. The fiction market is enormous and therefore has a tremendous financial upside if your work is rare, unique and deemed gifted by the publishing world, literary agents, and of course readers and future fans. Non-fiction is a far smaller market in general. A bestseller in the non-fiction world would barely get a fiction book on the notice charts. Even within fiction there are many different slants, such as writing historical fiction is not so very different from contemporary fiction; both need a sizzling plot and strong characters. But there are some aspects to historical fiction, which need more thought. Most readers want a strong sense of place in such books. If possible, you should have actual experience with these locales. Love the words and description of the story and make it very much your own voice. This will take your reader down a road filled with new experiences, that you are opening up for them. Your story should be filled with your own passion.

Don't get caught up in the concept of writers block. Writing is just like exercise; it requires daily work to stay in tiptop shape. Write every day, no matter how little, even though you feel your writing is not as good as you want it to be; ideas will continue to flow and it is easy to revise. I find using an outline format in MS Word very useful, it allows you to make changes and then view them. There are also several good inexpensive writers software tools. I use a product called Storyist. It catalogs my characters and my plots for me. It also organizes my writing elements that make a good story so that I can make sure I address the key items that make for a great book. A successful first chapter can be fast, slow, thoughtful, dramatic, but it will introduce you to a unique world and a distinct voice from which it is inseparable as the tone of the authors' voice. The voice may belong to a character or to the authors themselves, but within a page or two the reader will add their own perceived tone to the voice and therefore make it very personal to themselves.

The main advice for all writers – aspiring, emerging and/or established – is the same, you must sit down and write. A book can take a very long time to create, and it's too easy to get bogged down in the early stages, re-writing beginning sections rather than pressing forward with bold story parts that need refinement at a later time. There is no formula for writing a great book they are creations unique to each author. There are no rules to success. Success can be the actual accomplishment of having written the book for most. Most authors do not set out to write for a huge profit, they set out to tell their story burning inside them, their passion and need for expression is what drives them. A great book is one that you think is great and that is enough for most. Write the book that you yourself would like to read, not the book you think others want to read. I think the best advice I can give aspiring and emerging authors is to plan your novel and manuscript carefully, and get your work read. Building a support group of dedicated fans that will give you feedback is important, but so is developing a writing team. Writers today depend upon collaboration with other writing experts to grow and cultivate their craft. I have found that having niche group editors, all types of editors, illustrators, publicity and marketing folks that you can relate to are also essential if you want commercialization. I always used to tear into writing a new book without making a proper plan or synopsis; impatient to get down to the nuts and bolts of writing, but using a sound outline has made my writing easier and far more flexible to my actual creative process. Don't drive yourself nuts analyzing what is out there on the shelves already, or trying to spot the next trend, or trying to emulate your favorite author. Write the very book you would love to read, in your own voice, with your own style and driven by your own passion. This is what will make you successful and more important what will fulfill you in the end once it is completed. It is your art, if others desire it, then what a great compliment to you. My Mother-In-Law asked me one time, "Why do you think you can be an author? What if nobody else likes or reads your book?" She was quite concerned about my intent to write a book. My response was simple. "I am not writing this book for anyone else but for myself, if others do not choose to read it, I still feel I have done what I have always wanted to do." That is the advice I will leave for you if you choose to follow this noble path for yourself.

Now let me address the final remaining issue that seems to cloud many budding and aspiring authors thoughts and create quite a sense of being in a conundrum, whether to self-publish independently or go through the grueling process of finding a publisher, which most of the time also requires first finding a literary agent interested in representing you. This had so much emotion built into the subject when it is really no longer so difficult.

First, lets address the misnomer of the perceived stigma of being self-published or what is referred to as going with an Indie publishing house (independent usually print on demand publisher). There are thousands of highly successful Indie/Self-published authors and more emerging by the hour. The reason if very much related to my opening discussion in this chapter. Many authors, especially in the non-fiction realm are writing to their specific knowledge and niche audience, and that audience may not be large enough to deem a traditional publisher's investment. Nonetheless, the audience is large enough to make the author's work very highly valued and if it is good, very marketable within that audience niche. My own example is my initial writing career was focused on the niche industry of economic development. When I launched my first book, I had literally no competition in my audience space from within their ranks. It propelled by first book to iconic status. Even today my first book, "The Little Black Book of Economic Development," sells vibrantly within the field of my expertise. It continues nearly seven years after it's initial launch to be the most sought out book purchased by my fellow economic development practitioners. I recently decided that it deserved and needed an update so this year I wrote the updated second edition. Here is what is surprising the 2nd edition sells very well, but also continues to create sales for the first edition. Now my other books within this niche have a strong following and also sell well because of the niche audience I launched my book within. That is why there is no shame in self-publishing.

Also the concept of self-publishing is no longer a stigma because many accomplished and internationally renowned authors now own their own publishing company and then sell their books to the world, and to a publishing house as a completed and self-contained project. This means they have spent the time, money and energy to do all the normal inside the publisher duties and expenses at their own risk. This includes editing through all phases, developmental, polish, line and proof reads. The author has designed and paid for the book's layout both interior and exterior and also has designed their social media platform and website for distribution of news and information to the fan base and media. All of this decreases the traditional publishers exposure to financial risk and thus allows the author to gain additional royalty from the sale of the book.

This creates a new hybrid market for authors that have good work, one of both a self-published and totally inclusive expression of the authors work, and one linked to the traditional publisher for distribution to bookstores. Today the only advantage that traditional publishers have is their appetite to place books on shelves of bookstores. In this type of environment many of us authors are also carving out the digital rights to our works as a separate revenue stream that we hold onto for our own purposes. Why? Because most traditional publishers still want the author to take the time and expense of creating a social media platform and doing a good bit of self-marketing. If this is the case, then why not protect that effort as something that is your reward for the time and effort? It also, allows us as authors to negotiate a much more lucrative royalty agreement on e-books and audio books. In this market in the old fashioned traditional publishing world, an author might make 10% to 15% of a books list price. Then of course you must pay your literary agent 10% to 15% of those funds for representing you. If you go the route of self-publishing your work and focus primarily on the E-book distribution and audio distribution area, the only area you can impact for the most part in reality, you can increase your share of the royalty to 55% to 70% depending on who you choose to publish and distribute for you. This is a huge increase in the authors' revenue stream. Secondary to this in addition to the financial reward is the now proof you have to demonstrate to the traditional publishers of your books desirability. So, going the route of self-publishing and Indie Publishing if done properly can actually increase your odds of getting a traditional publishing contract. As with any business, writing is a business. You need a great literary legal expert to represent you when you get to the business of negotiating a publishing contract. If you choose the route of going only traditional publishing, your odds are severely decreased on actually getting published. Literary agents get thousands of requests for submissions per week, and 99.9% of those are not done properly according to their protocol and/or are not well written submissions and thus end up rejected. You have probably heard many stories of how most of our most beloved authors today, spent years searching for an agent and received hundreds of rejection letters. That is almost always the case. If that is your chosen path, patience, persistence and tenacity is absolutely required.

With the new social media tools of today, it is much easier to locate literary agents, literary attorneys and even publishers. I use the search tools on LinkedIn to compile lists of various types of professionals that I can connect with and then communicate with to build my own relationship and hopeful support for my work. You still have to learn about and follow their chosen protocols for contacting them, but it makes doing so much easier and quicker. Keeping lists of such contacts inside their system also allows you for fast paced distribution of news releases, updates, and fan comments. All these are essential to your author platform. Today without a proper social media and Internet platform you will not likely succeed. Taking time to master these tools and build a collection of your own resources in cyberspace is paramount to eventual success in your endeavors as an author. I have compiled my own list of my own ever-expanding resources to this regard; the list always evolves because our growth and research should be a continuous part of our author platform. Constantly expanding our contacts though emails, blog sites, LinkedIn, Facebook, YouTube, and other tools such as Twitter is not part of any successful authors toolkit.

Another major consideration is that if you follow my own advised hybrid model, you can still produce an original work in the style of your best or raw chosen expression by printing what is referred to in the industry as a ARC (advanced Reader

Copy) of your original work. The reason I like this route is that it allows you to preserve the story as you yourself most enjoy it, before the editors and literary agents begin to force or heavily suggest all the industry protocols upon you for size (page count) and (unnecessary details to the story) those detailed edits they believe are essential and necessary if you want to be published by a traditional publisher. This has less significance if you are not seeking a traditional publisher and simply want to publish your original work without such edits. By creating An Authors ARC you preserve your original work. BTW (by the way) serious book collectors many times collect such ARC's as their most prized members of their book collections, they are often more valuable to both the collector and the secondary resale market than the notion of Signed First Editions. Anytime a successful author creates a unique or perceived rare commodity it increases the value to their fans.

There is hope though, if you follow my guidelines for this path, you can exponentially increase your odds of being considered by an agent, and thus getting traditionally published. I cannot make a guarantee of your work getting published, in the end, which still depends on the quality of your work.

Don Allen Holbrook

DEVELOPING YOUR AUTHOR VOICE

CHAPTER 2

What the heck is a "voice"? By this, do editors and agents mean "style"? I do not think that is really the case. By voice, I think they mean a unique way of putting words together, but a unique sensibility, a distinctive flair and/or way of looking at the world, an outlook that enriches an author's reach within an audience. They want to read an author who is like no other and unique. An original as each of us as humans are by nature. It is a person with great standout qualities that resonate in their writing style. This is Your Voice.

How can you develop your own voice and understand that it is really your voice? To some extent it happens all by itself because it exists within you naturally already. Stories come from the subconscious and are surfaced by our writing and/or expression of them. This was how early man created our own human history by oral stories past down generation to generation. What drives you to write, to some extent, are your own unresolved inner conflicts and desires to express yourself and hopefully be heard? It is our ID as psychologists often state, our desire to be valued and feel appreciated and having made a mark on humanity, that drives it to the surface like molten lava at the core of your soul shooting to the top and pouring out through the volcano of your expression. Have you noticed your favorite authors have character types that recur in their works? Plot turns that feel familiar? Descriptive details that you would swear you have read before? That is the subconscious at work, and their normal voice of how they themselves see the scene of their own stories. But it also resonates within their audience.

You can facilitate voice by giving yourself the freedom to say things in your own unique way and not fearing how it comes out. You do not speak exactly like anyone else, you meet normally, why should you expect to write like everyone else? You become a great author by offering your readers something they can't get anywhere else, . . . you, and your unique perspective on the subject matter and/or story.

Which means you have to put yourself on your pages and see this story as if you were actually living it. Many authors become so immersed in their story they loose sight of actual reality at times and believe events that happened in the book happened in real life. That is when you know you need a break and some fresh air. You have to keep a grip on reality still to be successful, but it is that ability to get lost in your writing that makes awesome and world-renowned authors. This is what is known in the writing business as developing your voice. Voice isn't merely style and it is a sense of being. Style would be easy by comparison and could be recreated by many others. Style is watching your use of adjectives and doing a few flashy things with alliterations and careful edits. Style without voice is hollow and lacks true meaning and depth that reaches an audience. Voice is style, theme, personal observations, passion, beliefs, personal experiences, plus your own desired outcome. Voice is bleeding onto each page, and it can be a powerful, freeing and also very frightening naked experience of raw expression.

But your own voice is your future in writing and it is mandatory to being successful. Even though it is an art form of expression, it can be nurtured to the surface, so let's look at some techniques to help you.

1. Read Anything You Can and Become an Expert on Subject Matter...

It has been said by numerous experts in the writing industry that you cannot be a successful writer if you don't read yourself. That isn't opinion; that's fact because it relates to the experience of reading unto it's own. All writers read, and all good writers read a lot of stuff from many areas of interest. You cannot afford to be a book snob — don't write off any genre or type of book as being without redeeming qualities or lessons to teach you. The more you read, the more you will acquire a natural instinct about what works for you and why, and an equally compelling instinct for what doesn't and why. By reading you get first hand examples of how stories are put together, get a feel for how good novels are paced and plotted and how bad ones fall apart. This will inspire you to visualize your own stories. Reading is magic of a sort. It's your supply of ingenuity and innovation that supplies your imagination with fuel for writing.

2. Write Daily

You have to exercise your writing to become proficient at it. This means you have to write many times all different genres to become an expert at your own chosen genre.

3. Copy what has worked for others.

Your objective in finding your own voice is to loosen up your writing muscles by writing your OWN Version of work in someone else's voice, simply to shut up your inner critic. This can give you experience in how to switch voices in your own works.

I find staying connected to circles of writing resources such as journals, magazines and web groups to be a highly effective method for practicing on your craft.

4. Develop your own Back Story of Your thoughts

Don't just go through the motions of the most recent current events; instead look at your catalog of your own experiences and how you perceive those memories today. Example what did you learn from them? What would you have done differently today knowing what you know about the outcome and choices you had? This is a great source for your expression as a writer, do not over look these topics such as:

1. Childhood memories and how they impacted you
2. Dreams and nightmares and any linkages you feel.
3. If I found a genie in bottle what would I wish (3 things).
4. If money were not an issue, what would I buy and do...
5. If I could have anything what would it be and why?
6. What scares me and how do I avoid it or deal with it
7. Things you have found that seem mysterious or not usual
8. What do you find sexy and why... who embodies that to you
9. What would your favorite food or meals be if you could have anything you want to eat for a week
10. Describe the best times of your life and who they were

with and how you felt during that time

You can come up with endless other topics for this list too. Use this list as a trigger point for how you describe and launch your own characters or expression of your own unique writing voice. Chances are if this interests you it will captivate many others just as well.

5. Challenge your preconceptions.

You don't know everything about yourself. You only think you do. The more you trust yourself to write without correction, the more you'll discover that you're a lot deeper and more interesting and more complex than you imagined.

But you'll find out a lot about yourself by pushing some of your own buttons, too, and I recommend that from time to time you do. If you're a staunch Republican, write an essay from inside the head of a liberal Democrat who is in favor of the thing you most despise, whether it is entitlement spending or gun control or free abortions on demand. If you're strongly science-oriented, write from inside the head of a modern mystic who makes a living as a professional psychic, and who strongly and passionately believes in his or her work. If you're strongly religiously oriented, write from inside the head of a person who loathes all religion, and has good reason for doing so.

Your job in this exercise is to **become**, although only temporarily, the thing that most frightens, angers, or bewilders you. To do it right, you have to allow your enemy to convince you of his rightness — you cannot allow yourself to convince him. For example, the strongly Christian writer cannot have the character he is writing experience a conversion to Christianity or see the error of his ways — he must, instead, have the agnostic prove to himself that he is **right** in his choice to be agnostic. This gets us out of our element and thus creative.

I'll tell you right now that this is some of the toughest writing that you'll ever do. Don't try it when you're tired or cranky or when you have a headache — you'll probably get one from this particular exercise even if you felt great beforehand. But do take the leap and do this. It is the absolute best way (if you play fairly) that I've ever found to start developing characters that aren't either transparent versions of yourself or pathetically weak straw men that you can triumph over as villains.

6. Dare to be dreadful, passionate, and risky...

When you're finding your writers voice, you're going to be doing a lot of experimenting outside of your comfort zone. Some of what you writing will be lousy and some will shock you and amaze you at the same time. Candor is your friend in these matters. I feel that the only way you'll get any good as a writer and published author if you allow yourself to put whatever comes out in your expressions from your mind down on the page without fretting over how to phrase the prose of yourself or not embarrass yourself by being so naked in your candor. You have to take risks of expression or you are no better than all those that will remain unpublished. You have to teach yourself to step outside of your comfort zone and take enormous risks of expression on your pages or you will not be a great writer!

During this time it isn't the time to be aiming for calculating how commercial viable is my writing. When your internal writing coach or sensor tries to switch on, you have to ignore it or you will fail as an author that writes with a meaningful and passionate voice.

7. Complacency destroys Writers and Being Fearless Inspires Writers.

If you're comfortable, then you are not outside of the box and you are now in the herd of folks that will never be published and/or heard. Writing excellent is done from a position of discomfort otherwise you will never say anything worthwhile.

The opposite of this is of course being fearless, not without fear, but rather one who writes and expresses their feelings in spite of their fears. Courage is the conviction to face your fears and still function towards the outcomes you desire.

At the heart of everything that you've ever read that moved you, touched you, changed your life, there was a writer's fear. And a writer's determination to say what he had to say in spite of that fear is what defines them.

Your voice is born and nurtured from a lot of words and a lot of hard work and tireless effort in spite of how it will be perceived by others; it is your natural expression of your own passions. Voice will make your soul bleed, it will scare you, it will amaze you and it will wake you up to so many of your suppressed feelings and thoughts that it will liberate you as person. You already have a voice. It's wonderful and it's unique to you, it's the voice of a best seller should be your only mindset. Your job as an author is to guide it from the darkest of the dark places at your core and let it find the light of day though expression.

Don Allen Holbrook

CREATING A WRITING FORMAT

CHAPTER 3

Writing does require building your own format or style for how you will organize your rough draft prior to any real editing. I divide this into two major steps. First the book overview, later we will use this to develop or pitch or synopsis for use in promotion. It starts with just some simple basics, and all of these are subject to revision and changes until the day you hit, send manuscript for production.

Production Infrastructure:

Name of your book

Possible Subtitles

Author(s) and anyone you feel might be a good contributor to your work:

Basic Description of the Theme and Content of the Story: (What, where, why and what if statements). I like to call these your WWW's. Then do the next level of your message, to determine your audience. (What do I want them to understand or take away from this work, why will they bother to read it, and what will they learn from this or what will resonate with my audience from this work, why does it matter to them?)

Plot Development Genre: (is this fictional or non-fiction)... this creates the divided highway of how much detail and factual and concise effort you must place into your work, and how you will prepare for supporting your work.

Basic Characters Description(s) and/or Topic of the Book if Non-fiction;

Opening Pilot Concept (4-8 paragraphs) no more than two pages: Think of this as your elevator pitch something that will guide you as an executive summary to a full fledged report... it is the soup not all the ingredients.

Major Story Beat Sheet Points: (Each is a plot story example sub-story element). The best way to write most books I have found is to create a ten to fifteen point list of every major event and/or plot point I want to go into more detail upon later. Then write just a few paragraphs about how you see each point being summarized. You can add additional points if fifteen are not enough.

Conclusion of Ending Description: (4-8 paragraphs): This is the meat of what you wish to be the findings or outcomes to your story. Why did someone take all the time to read this? What did they discover and what makes it important and how do we know it is conveyed properly? How do you feel you will know if your writing is successful in this conclusion by your own expression?

Next you have to go about doing the administrative functions. They should include all of the following if you want to properly protect your work, which are your own unique intellectual rights.

Administrative Actions:

File with the Screen Writers Guild of America West

File with the Patent Office Under Copyrights

Set-up a Library of Congress Number

Create your own ISBN and make sure you control it (Universal)

Set up an account with Your Chosen Publisher for publication

Now you are ready to commence drafting your notes and thoughts.

THE ART OF GETTING HELP

CHAPTER 4

This is a special chapter dear new friend. I get asked many times about how to go about writing a book, getting it published and then fulfilling what many hold as a lifelong dream of being a published author. Let me start off by making the following observations and then I will give you my own quick guide to getting started and getting this completed. It was for this reason that I sat down and organized myself and wrote this actual book. You could say the entire essence of this book was derived from the elements and demands I have found for this chapter during my own life.

First, all authors use editing teams, and professional writing teams and they pay for such services out of their own pocket or from their book advances if their manuscript is picked up by a major publishing house. In order to get an advance on your book the manuscript it has to be optioned by the publishing house. Normally this is a very difficult task in itself. The best way to accomplish this if this is your choice is to get a literary agent. Getting a literary agent is almost like hunting for a needle in a haystack as well. They are very picky and do not

take many unproven authors and/or emerging authors on
board. To submit to a literary agent you have to provide them
with a pitch letter (I recommend getting one professionally
written for you) and then provide them with a short example
of your writing style and hopefully from your book such as the
first chapter of first 10-15 pages.

Now with this said, let's talk about what many choose as the
first and most effective approach to getting yourself published.
I believe the most practical route is to self-publish and self-
market your first book. Let me discuss why this is still a very
respectable and cost-effective route for getting yourself
published.

First, you have lots of choices, but I would recommend you do
not spend money on the entire self-publishing guru's out there.
They will way over charge you for what I believe you can do far
more cost-effective through the resources I will provide you
with short white paper on this subject. In my nearly ten years
publishing and writing books I have learned a great deal and I
am passing this experience onto you as a professional courtesy.
What ends up happening is you can publish your book and
then market it to your friends and contacts and build a strong

reader base. You will make money on the sales from the booksellers, such as Amazon and Barnes & Noble. Amazon is by far the best route for self-publishers as they have very easy to use tools for you to use as you progress through the book writing, editing, and cover design and marketing aspects.

Now let's go through the process of defining how to go about writing the book and getting it edited.

Preparation Before You Write the Book is Critical!

Before you publish the book do two very important steps:

First go to the Screen Writers Guild of America West and enter your description of your book project in their database and pay the $25 fee to protect your intellectual rights.

http://www.wga.org/

Then submit a copyright for your book with the US patent office.

http://www.copyright.gov/document.html

Next, I recommend you set up an account with Amazon self-publishing and then follow their book process: The Amazon book publishing company is called Create Space, here is the link; https://www.createspace.com/

You can choose whichever publisher you like for this purpose.

Self Publishing vs. Traditional Publishing:

First thing you must realize is that there is no negative stigma to self-publishing. In fact, unless you are highly acclaimed fiction writer you may very well be forced down this avenue just because nobody will take a chance on you or your first manuscript. Second thing to realize is that if you build an audience for your books they will follow your new books and become a built in audience to purchase your books in the future. This makes self-publishing far more lucrative to you as an author. The self-publishing route will enable you to determine your book price and platforms, such as printed, e-book, audio, etc. You will also make a considerable amount more per book in the self-publishing avenue. Depending on your pricing anywhere from 50% to 70% of your retail price. If you build a fan base of several thousand people this could mean the difference in paying for all the professional costs you will have to launch your book and have it laid out, proof read, edited and a professional cover and typesetting expert do the polish work. Just as in any other business your first impression is critical. So do it right and use professionals and you will build a positive and professional fan base.

Traditional publishers will probably not give you a royalty advance unless you have so dazzled them that they feel it merits taking a risk on a new artist. Even then the average advance might be $10,000.00 and they will charge you for all the services I mentioned above at their cost with overhead and profit margin. So, for you to make any money on your book you would probably need to sell about $100,000.00 worth of books to recoup that advance for them at their prices before you started seeing any monies to you on the sale end of the book. That is a pretty hefty projection and thus why most first time authors do not garner such advances.

First of all doing this yourself will more than likely if you do not spend money on professional caliber services produce a book that is not marketable and not very reader friendly... you have to pay for professional services to get published if you want a high quality end product you will be proud of.

Follow their guidelines step by step and you can purchase the services you need and I highly recommend you purchase the following services:

1.) Editing comprehensive package and polish editing
2.) Cover Design package
3.) Interior Type Setting and Page Layout
4.) EBook set up and creation for electronic book distribution
5.) Distribution world wide (Ingram and Baker Taylor)
6.) Press release design and set up
7.) Select the Universal Copyright that allows you to change it to another publishing house in other words pay for it, don't accept their free one or you are stuck with CreateSpace in your publication distribution chain forever. Don't cheap out. It is normally about $99.00 for your own ISBN and another $49.00 for the Library of Congress submission and number assignment.
8.) I recommend you splurge and get a professional video trailer for your book as well with voiceover to make it unique and impactful. It really sets your book apart and allows you to showcase it on

YouTube, Flicker and other video social media resources.

9.) Set up a blog about your book at Wordpress.com that is a great way to market it to your friends and contacts on LinkedIn and Facebook. You need to get savvy about social media if you want to become successful at self-promotion.

10.) Set up a professional Authors website with social media links to Facebook, (public figure) setting for authors and a group on LinkedIn for your fans.

Now you have all the tools to publish your book and become a paid published author. There is no real distinction between self-published and Published by a major book publishing house other than the breadth of distribution. In addition, getting your book self-published may draw attention to it and help you become discovered... this is a discussion where there are many who feel it does not and many who feel it does...in the end I believe it is better to be published than not.

There is a good resource you can pay to have your manuscript critiqued and then given advice on how to improve upon your writing, story development and characters or facts at the following resource agency:

http://www.scribendi.com/service/manuscript_critique?s_kw cid=TC%7C22090%7C%2Bbook%20critique%7C%7CS%7Cb %7C22749861819&gclid=CK6t-trViLECFSgbQgodSE_IWA

I choose the software tool called Storyist for my own book writing projects because it seems very robust and user friendly. Here is a link to that software if you choose to use professional software, which I highly recommend. Remember you are investing in making the most use of your time and it is simply a powerful leg up over those that try to do this the old fashioned way. The software is very reasonably priced at about $59.00 for a one-time fee to download it to your computer. It also works on other platforms including IPad and such. http://storyist.com/index.html

If you choose to submit your manuscript to literary agents here is a website full of great links to most of the accomplished literary agents:

http://wlwritersagency.com/index.html?gclid=CI-R26nFybACFagaQgodoBFRYg&utm_expid=47838522-7

http://www.firstwriter.com/Agents/

http://www.agentquery.com/

Don't be surprised if you get a zillion rejections... all writers go through this trauma. It can take years or months to find a good literary agent that will represent your work. They should not charge you to do so. If they want a fee for such representation then they are not in my opinion a true literary agent but more than likely a publicist. I can give you a few publicists that I find to be very credible if you want to pay for exposure.

There are new tools that can also help you target a query letter to the literary agents. I recommend you consider using such services. The one I personally use and recommend is Writer's Relief submission services. The cost dependent upon how many you have them send out. Varies from basic services for about $150.00 for research only up to about $450.00, which I highly recommend. The full service contains Query letter, proof reading and creating your submission packet about 10-15 pages of your book both hard copy and electronic versions and picking the top 25 markets where you are most likely to get traction and/or get noticed by an agent. They also include submission to 25 literary agents on your behalf. Resubmission is about $380 for the next set of 25 literary agents. They will track all your submissions for you so you know status and whom you have targeted along with any feedback. This is a huge time saver and well worth your money and effort.

http://www.writersrelief.com/

I believe in using paid resources in your initial first efforts, because in essence you are paying to be professionally educated and not at the expense of misrepresenting or poorly positioning your manuscript. It has been through the use of these various services that I have grown much more capable as my own CEO of my Author efforts. Being an author at least a successful published author means you are the Captain of your own destiny and of your own unique ship. Thus you are whether you like it or not the CEO of YOU, Inc.

Here is a good article on what a publicist does for you:

http://www.publishersweekly.com/pw/by-topic/columns-and-blogs/soapbox/article/47737-do-you-know-what-a-book-publicist-does-.html

Here are publicists that I believe in my opinion seem very credible;

http://www.bookpr.com/aboutbookpublicitybookpromotion.htm

http://www.maryglenn.com/services.html

http://anniejenningspr.com/

I have used Annie Jennings and she does what she says she will do... you have to have a pretty good economic situation to get on the big networks, but she can get you on national media if you pay for the services. It is very likely she and some others like her can get you on many local, regional and national radio shows, possibly national and regional television and even newspapers and magazines, but you must pay to be part of that form of success. They run many specials. I have found a very reputable non-fiction literary agent/publicist resource is Keller Media in Los Angeles; she can take a newbie author from soup to nuts for under a thousand dollars. Wendy Keller is a serious literary agent with a mission to help others get noticed and published. She has a track record to back up all her claims, so I have found her to be very reputable.

http://www.kellermedia.com/consulting/

Also, you may want to join some writer's resources such a free newsletter and subscribe to the Writers Digest quarterly magazine. These are great places to get ideas and resources about your journey as an author.

http://www.writing-world.com/newsletter/index.shtml

http://www.writersdigestshop.com/?cid=3&gclid=CPOFj6SA4 7ICFQXhQgodazoA_Q

I am a subscriber to the Writers Digest printed edition and I get their email newsletters. I find them to be very helpful.

I also recommend that you purchase the Writers Digest Guide to Literary Agents, which is published annually for about $20.50 it is written by Chuck Sambuchino, the largest blog regarding literary agents on the web.

http://www.amazon.com/Guide-Literary-Agents-Chuck-Sambuchino/dp/1599635976

Now if you choose to use a professional Ghostwriter either to take your verbal or emailed notes and turn it into a readable book this is a very good way to start out and learn how to actually design and write your first book. It is not a necessary step but many first time authors do so. Here is a little secret, most professional authors have a team of ghost writers and editors that help them craft their book into the best outcome, so there is no shame in using such services. Not many authors write every word of their books, but most supervise and comment on what gets into the final edition. There is no shame in getting written assistance in your expression. Most successful authors do so; just look at their books acknowledgment pages if you need proof of my statement.

Here are some ghostwriting resources if you should happen to choose this route. Again ghost writing can cost approximately $.08 to .22 cents per word or more for creative works depending on the appetite of the ghostwriter at the time for some economic relief and according to their own skill sets. The better writers will command that top number of $.10 to .22 cents per word. The average manuscript is between 250,000 to 500,000 words (250 to 500 pages). So ghostwriting can get quite expensive. Editing even after the manuscript is ghost written is an essential next step and will cost another $.02 to .10 per word for a complete comprehensive edit and polish of your manuscript.

Here are some good websites to scout for ghostwriters:

http://www.rainbowriting.com/ghostwriter.htm

http://www.associationofghostwriters.org/find_ghostwriter.html

So as you can see a committed author will have in many cases well over $10,000 tied up in their book production. This is not a hobby for those that are cheapskates. But, the pride and value of being a published author with an exceptionally well-written book to most of us is well worth the investment. Plus you pay this out over what is normally a 12-month to 18-month process so it won't necessarily break your budget if you prepare yourself for it and budget for this over a reasonable time period.

If you want to turn your manuscript into a screenplay this is another very comprehensive process and again, I would recommend you seek professional help.

There are some essentials you need to have a marketable screen play.

1.) Book to Film Screenplay Treatment (this describes the concept and budget considerations and market target audience venue to potential producers and directors).

2.) Screenplay Beat Sheet- an overview of the highlights of your screenplay best scenes to draw attention to the quality of the story.

3.) Screenplay Pitch Letter- this is the marketing letter you will utilize to actually attract the producer (the person responsible for developing the movie funding and the business agent for the production and marketing of the movie to the distribution outlets and studios for revenue) and the director (the person in charge of creating the film and getting it into final format for distribution and sale, they also will work with the Producer to decide on talent to use in the movie, locations, etc.)

4.) The actual screenplay. Don't overspend on the first version, as this will be rewritten at least once if not several times by the final producers and directors by their own preferred screenplay writers. Just get a screenplay written so you have something to sell to the interested parties besides a concept.

5.) A Video short of the screenplay can be used if produced to compete in major film festivals and this can draw attention to your project in a very credible manner.

Again, this process can run from about $7,000 to well over $25,000 if you manage it correctly… paying more than that for these services at this stage is in my opinion a waste of time and money. Most screenplay options will sell for $10,000 to $50,000, depending on the quality of the product and appetite of the Producer and Director for the project.

Here are some credible screenwriter resources that can assist you in this process from start to finish in my opinion:

http://hstrial-stewartproductio.homestead.com/index.html

http://erickmertzwriting.com/

If you want an awesome cover artist and/or screenplay poster developed I would recommend Eric Hollander, he did my cover for the 9th Templar and is an award winning New York Times cover and screen poster artist. Check out his work here:

https://www.facebook.com/erik.hollander1?fref=ts

Now you have the majority of the infrastructure you need to understand in order to create your book, publish it and promote it professionally. Each book is what I refer to as a passion project. They are works of art and can take from a short while to a lifetime to achieve, depending on your own pace and how you choose to invest both your own time and money into such an endeavor.

Now for my final comments on the actual writing of the story or manuscript as most of you have asked me for assistance on in the past or if you are receiving this PDF, you have asked me to give you some advice currently. Remember this is free advice and based on my own experiences and knowledge. What I have assembled for you in this newsletter has taken me over 7 years to assemble on my own through my own trial and error. But I have managed to get 10 books published and I have 3 additional fiction projects that are written at this time that I intend to publish once I get the final screenplay elements contracted and funded. I am starting on my 11th book (non-fiction) as I write this for you today. I enjoy writing immensely. I hope it will be equally as rewarding for each of you.

Here is my basic advice on how to get started writing your book idea. This template is laid out in good detail in the previous Chapter 3.

First, follow this template and you will be further ahead than you will believe when you are finished and it won't take nearly as long to produce your book either.

1.) Write the Title and your thoughts on what the book is generally about (the premise) and the genre (fiction, non-fiction, biography, historical, Children's story, etc.)

2.) Now write the 15-20 main points you want to make in your book. These should be one to two sentence topical statements.

3.) Now go back and write two to three paragraphs under each topical statement to fully describe your thoughts on those main points. Make this line spaced at 1.5 and 12 font in New Times Roman (this is standard book creation layout formatting).

4.) Now you have a general book outline and it will be somewhere in the 40 to 80 page length content... you will be surprised how fast these pages add up.

5.) Now go back and add any additional detail you want to each topic to bring it to the full clarity you want.

6.) If this is a fictional book do an outline of who each of the characters will be, their name, background, role in the book (hero, villain, sidekick, lover, supporting role, etc.)

7.) Next, do the sequential chapter outline of how you see the book progressing through these major topics or story points. Lay them in a sequence that makes sense to you and so the story flows in your own mind

Now you have the major elements necessary to go through the writing guidelines I have laid out for you previously in this newsletter starting with developmental editing of your story and such with the various services above.

There are also some professional writers software resources you may want to purchase that can help your organize your writing style and final product.

Here are some software resources I think are useful and cost-effective.

http://www.writersstore.com/software/creative-writing-and-journaling?cid=1820&gclid=CLbI-cKO47ICFal7Qgod3VEA-w

Personally, I do not use these software packages but that is up to your own individual needs and taste in how you want to progress your project without other professional help or intervention on a fee basis. I do know that many writers do utilize such software to keep themselves organized and to get assistance on the creative process. As I have said before, this is up to your own self-assessment of your needs. If you use this software in my opinion you still need to use the aforementioned fee based editorial services and cover design services, etc. This additional software is just a tool to assist you in your own creativity and organizational process for your book project.

As I have told many folks (those that want my advice on this subject) I believe everyone has a unique story or book within them, but most will not do what it takes to make this idea come to fruition as a reality.

If you would like me to read your story and provide comments I may do so on a case-by-case basis. This may seem too commercial but my own time is very valuable to me. I have taken the time to write this guide for you as a free contribution to all of my friends and colleagues that have chosen to consider such an undertaking. If you would like my further advice I will have to charge you for my services. For example to read and provide comments on a book idea I charge a flat fee of $250.00, which must be paid in advance of my providing any feedback. If you wish to retain me for such services simply email and arrange for payment and provide me with your manuscript. I will of course sign a confidentiality agreement not to disclose your idea to anyone.

Lastly, I have not provided you with the most of the names of my own writing team, producer, director and others directly involved with me on my projects, because they are very private folks and I did not feel they would want the publicity necessarily, without first seeking their permission to do so. I will provide this information to you on a case-by-case basis only after I have discussed your needs with my own team members and contacts personally to see if they have any interest in speaking with you directly. I am sure you can appreciate my own need to preserve my infrastructure and their own need for discretion and privacy on such matters.

FREE ADVICE VERSUS PAID

CHAPTER 5

The old saying past down from generation to generation is exactly correct here. If you really want professional and meaningful advice you have to be prepared to pay for such advice. Good or great advice from very credible resources with excellent track records and references are worth their proverbial weight in gold. They will save you hours of frustration and anguish over things that in the end you may not have any or much control over in the first place.

I believe the major issue and one of the other reasons for writing this book is to determine some proven shortcuts for those of us seeking such advice from those of us that have already taken such advice. Being willing to collaborate and cooperate with your fellow authors and those that are aspiring to do so, can be very fulfilling personally. Plus professionally it is part of the entire concept of paying it forward. If none of us took effort to record our experiences and provide them to those of you in search and need of them, we ourselves might not have received the assistance we needed. This effort is for all of us to develop our own resource list. If none of us took the time to do so we would not find such needed assistance ourselves when we desire it. It is only when we all take the effort to be useful to each other that we improve the plight for all of us.

Free advice can sometimes be inspiring and useful, but many times it is not from someone that has much credibility and/or mastery of the subject we are actually in need of exploring, therefore these type conversations can be open to a huge amount of personal opinion with no substantive experience from which the opinion is being based upon.

The bigger concern today on paid advice is are we really purchasing something useful and relevant and/or is it just some hyperbole from someone peddling their services and products on the Internet with no real meat or actual in-depth value to us as authors. Unfortunately the list of sources that are not very useful and/or very over priced is longer than any of us can track and growing exponentially by the day.

Checking references and actually speaking with past clients is essential to anyone that chooses to spend their hard earned money on such services. I wish I could just point you to everyone that is credible but that would be absurd and far to fluid for me to record in a written format. My book has at least compiled a fairly lengthy list of those I have had discussions and utilized some of their services from in the past and/or am doing so currently. Even when your vendor is credible though, remember that there is no guaranteed that their efforts will succeed to the level of your own expectations. Anyone who makes such promises should be viewed with a very skeptical eye. In the next chapter I will discuss my own creation of an actual business case for the promotion of my own non-fiction book, "The Next America-Moving Beyond a Fragile Economy," and my debut fiction novel, "The Ninth Templar." I felt by allowing you to read my own-recorded thoughts from my own journal and cataloging of my efforts it might help some of you sort through this same exercise for yourselves. I hope you find this useful. As is always the case, I am attempting to increase your options for consideration, not directly influence your actual choices in such matters. There is no affinity or marketing royalty kick back paid (direct or indirect) to me for my thoughts on each of the services and vendors discussed.

BUILDING YOUR BUSINESS CASE
(SELLING YOUR BOOK TO READERS)

CHAPTER 6

Executive Summary:

Your business case is very personal and should be simple to convey and understand by most anyone reading it, the KISS principle (Keep It Short & Sweet). It is highly biased to your own unique approach... after all you are writing this partly as an exercise to convince yourself to invest your hard earned money into YOU! If you think it sounds incredulous and unbelievable then it probably is. It needs to be based upon realistic goals and objectives and also should be a format for tracking what has worked and/or not for future reference and reconsideration. Anyone who does not approach the business side of why they write and how they would like to be rewarded not only personally but also monetarily will probably not succeed at commercialization of their book to the markets. One key point is to remember that your book needs to be available in all E-book formats, audio format and through Itunes for IPad. This is essential to your brand distribution.

Example: "The Next America-Moving Beyond a Fragile Economy"

The Intention of my existing books are to create a niche in the field of non-fiction for my work as an economic development economist and the rebuilding of local communities in order to prosper in the changing economic landscape of the 21st Century. This platform is to be utilized for the promotion of my self-spoken consulting to primarily local chambers of commerce and economic development agencies. This publication plan will further supports my efforts to create paid speaking engagements, a digital (virtual platform built on annual and/or monthly subscriptions) and the sale of my books and additional consulting services.

My Fiction Novel Example: "The Ninth Templar"

The intention of my new fiction thriller novels is to create a specific niche with the general public and build fan base by developing readers and grow a niche following of avid fans that will create sufficient demand for my novels to become recognized as best sellers on the New York Times List and international book retailers lists. It is my desire for my thriller novels to become published and then distributed in a formal format with a well-recognized traditional publisher. This process is meant to develop me as a world-renowned and recognized author that creates exciting books for readers. The ability for me to position this as a book to film concept is highly important to me. Therefore much of my work has been done to position my intellectual assets so that this three-step process is placed into action. My initial debut of the fiction novel may require some self-publication promotion strictly in the E-book format. I want to preserve the printed format for a traditional publisher relationship. If I do not uncover a very well respected literary agent within my efforts in last quarter of 2013 and first quarter of 2014 I may choose to continue forward with my own self-publication efforts.

All of these considerations are realistic and based upon the likely reality that much of what I try will need to be constantly adapted and modified in the end to become successful.

Pre-production:

Fiction book- (9th Templar)- This book remains necessary for at a minimum at least an additional developmental edit by a very well seasoned fiction editor that has done work on the New York Times best selling list for other authors. I have two editors in mind. Their fees are basically $7500.00 for the edits and notes with recommendations. After which I will use my own editor to make suggested changes. Then upon completion of the developmental edit I will proceed to the line edit and then the polish-edit and then the type set edit for book interior design. Cost for this service is expected to run approximately $1600. The book will be professionally laid out for E-book format in all digital services for another $150. The cover (back cover mostly) needs to be finished and I expect that will run approximately $900. In addition I will design a book club discussion guide for $350 for this book with novel publicity using their Pavarti Tyler.

Literary Agent Representation:

It is my intention to seek literary agent representation for the fiction book prior to any final expenditure on the actual manuscript. This also will allow me to gain their own unique input for my own use. I am giving the agent quest approximately 6 months before moving to a plan B.

It is important that we establish our own patience factor into our business case but always be prepared to modify and adjust this expectation based on learned experiences from your trial by fire or practice.

I intend on using a professional Query service called Writers Relief. They will produce the query letter and send out 25 per month for two months for $450. They also will create a one-page leave behind. I intend to have their query letter reviewed by Writers Digest services for another $80. The cost to send this out to agents is budgeted at $200 per month for six months so approximately $1200. This should commence immediately while promoting the Non-fiction book as part of **Step One,**

Production Plan:

This is where the rubber meets the road, where the real trial by exposure starts to take very significant meaning.

Non-Fiction book, The Next America- first, I will send a copy to Cedar Fort for traditional publishing consideration. Then it will require reformatting into a universal E-book digital format so it will be available to all Ereaders. This will cost me approximately $150. I also need to have the E-book reformatted for the interior to digital E-book and this will cost approximately $300. This is **Step One: Since the book is already on Amazon I decided to promote it exclusively first through Kindle Nation for $199 and Bookdaily for $49.00 and also move to Ebookit Press for $199 and $195 with a press release campaign. I am including bloggers next for $199 through Pump Up Promotions to hit top 20 bloggers. This push will get me quick exposure! Next I will move to Net Galley for $349 for two months ads.**

I also plan on developing a video trailer for the book for promotional purposes. The cost of the video trailer could run as high as $2200 or as low as $400. This is **Step Two:**

 The book will require a new author bio $50, and the creation of a book tour and book club discussion guide for $350. This is **Step Three:** The book shall require a new website to promote the concept which I anticipate the author website to run approximately $1250 to $1500. This is **Step Four**:

 I intend to use a promotional virtual book tour with bloggers in the next step to make it more recognized and search engine optimized. This is **Step Five:**

Fiction book, The 9th Templar- will require considerable more planning than the already finished non-fiction book. The book needs to be produced in E-book format for promotion as an advanced reader edition in only E-book format to build awareness and media buzz. I am leaning towards Bookbaby with Baker Taylor for this production about $395. I may use Friessen publishing plan if I self-publish which is turnkey for $4995. It will require the production of both paperback and hardcover editions and the ability to distribute through Ingram and Baker Taylor for bookstore orders and return policies. My entire game plan is to find a traditional book publisher possibly Cedar Fort to distribute the book and I will underwrite the production and marketing efforts as my part of the partnership. The 9th Templar needs six fine art illustrations and I have budgeted $250 each for them so a total of $1500 to $2,000.

Post Production Marketing & Advertising:

Non-fiction- Create the marketing plan and advertising plan for a major push into the media markets for exposure. The use of a professional service such as Authoright is possible for placement of the initial press release, at a fee of $3095. (This should be last marketing test). The first low hanging fruit marketing would be to follow up with a blitz on the bloggers and book reviews by hiring services as follows; Kindle Nation-SEO/FB $349, Bookdaily blast (3) months $199, Kindle nation email blast $297 for three months. Next I would move to book bloggers for $200. Bookbub is a good service for $600. This is **Step Six:** Another service is Ebookit Prweb $390 and Erelease is $499 for guaranteed placement in over 100 media outlets. Then there is Ebookit, which hits all the media for $195 plus the press release design is $295 overpriced. This is **Step Seven:** This next step would be to hire someone to maximize Goodreads for my book. That cost should be about $250. This is **Step Eight:** Once the impact of these techniques has been benchmarked and reviewed the option is to either commence the steps six and seven over again and/or go to Authoright or Resultsource for their intensive marketing launch service.

This is **Step Nine**:

Step Ten: Review the impact of all of steps six through nine and evaluate which steps are most effective and cost-effective and consider modifications to next marketing push. One additional step can be to place the book on sale and do book signing in the Las Vegas market at Barnes & Noble, Independent booksellers and the Airport.

Fiction Book- Video Trailer will run about $2200. I also plan on using the Enovelreview service for $175.00 for three months. I will create the media blast with ebookit for $195, plus $295. I will use the Writers Digest service for the press release for the others. Send out news release through book blast on Bookdaily for $197 for three months, Bookbub for $750, kindle nation for $349 FB/SEO and daily deal for $99 plus Email blast for $199 and the Thriller of the Week for $529 all on Kindle nation. I will employ book bloggers for $400 two months. Website for the book should run approximately $1500 fully optimized to my blog and book sales. A good social media optimization through Pavarti Tyler is $150 for each

Twitter and Facebook. The E-book format will run $399 plus the production at Bookbuddy for IPad is $199.

Once sales production reaches 30,000 digital books I will invest in the screenplay for sale to a film producer/director. Kathy Krantz has the best price at $5000 turn key. **Step eleven.**

Publicity Milestones & Goals

Non-fiction book- placement in top media outlets such as New York Times, Washington Post, Minneapolis Star Tribune, Dayton Daily News, Las Vegas Review Journal, Houston Tribune, Los Angeles Times, San Francisco Times, and Wall Street Journal. Interviews on PBS-Radio and Television. I would like to generate at least 100 reviews of my book on Amazon and Barnes & Noble in total. I would like to build a 10,000 plus fan base on Facebook for the book in my Author's section. Generate at least 10,000 twitter followers for the book. **Step twelve:** consider pay for placement services in these venues for promotional purposes.

Fiction Book- Placement in New York Times, Washington Post, and Wall Street Journal under books to consider. Interviews by major news outlets perhaps ten that are interested in the story behind the book. At least one interview on PBS- Radio or Television. Invitations to sell the book at major independent booksellers and national chains such as Costco and Barnes & Nobel is crucial. Generate 100,000 fans on Facebook with likes for my book and another 10,000 on twitter.

Sales

What is important in this exercise is that you establish your necessary return on investment for the expenditure of your monies. If you do not know your sales quota you will not know if your book is actually profitable from a hard money sense. It may be emotionally profitable but not monetarily profitable. A very real circumstance and/or outcome of this exercise is to determine your bleed factor, how long will you choose to invest and at what level of investment, and at what point has the book either succeeded and thus further investment is prudent and profitable, and/or further investment is not advised or at least your approach to such sales generation is clearly failing to produce your desired and expected profits. Remember sales do not come in methodical manners normally but rather normally they can come in heaps and floods or trickles over a prolonged time period of effort and then due to the viral nature of the Internet and social media, they can take off like a rocket without warning. There are plenty of stories of both success and defeat to support this scenario. Only you can determine your patience and investment threshold.

Non-fiction book has a goal of selling **5800 E-books** during the initial campaign over 12 months. Once this is accomplished my goal is to boost the E-book sales to an additional **6000 sales** so that the book become visible to the media and general public on major book lists and continues to generate profit for me as the author. My print sale goal is to sell approximately 1000 books in paperback into major book retailers. The audio book should continue to be promoted to sell approximately 200 per month once the book is discovered and e-book sales of 5800. My first year-book sales goal therefore would look like this; **5,800 E-books, 1,000 print books** and over **2400 audio books** for a total book sales quota of **9200** books through all formats with an over-all average price point of $3.99 each. My <u>over-all sunk cost</u> in TNA is approximately **$10,000** complete turnkey. Profit Goal is **$11,900.00 at 55% Net Profit**. Do not move to the Fiction book until non-fiction E-book is proven. During the promotion year I will be building the infrastructure to prepare the 9th Templar for release in late 2014 by Christmas is my goal.

My **fiction book** is a much more aggressive plan. It has significantly more expense involved in the actual production in order for me to reach breakeven and eventual profitability. My <u>sunk cost in this book is approximately $45,000</u> with all costs included with the final developmental edit (David Compton or Laurie Rosin). Therefore the sales need to be much higher to substantiate my ROI. My E-book plan and trailer will include the fiction novel, The 9th Templar plus the Theoretical History of the Knights Templar coffee table book. These shall be marketed in tandem. The E-book sales shall target **<u>16,188 books to break even</u>**. Once this is accomplished the push is to get the book over **25,000 e-book sales** within the first year of promotion. In addition I intend to push the audio sales so that it generates approximately 500 sales per month to make first year digital sales of **30,000 books**. The goal **for E-book/Digital Profit is $20,700** based on a price point of $3.99 each and 55% profits from sales. Once this is accomplished my focus will be on printed book distribution through the retail chains. My goal is to get 20,000 books sold through this format. The second printing should target another 25,000 books for promotion focusing highly on the airport kiosks for this promotion. I will not go to printed production until digital sales reach 30,000 units. My goal is to get this book on the New York Times best-seller list within 12 months.

Platform

Once the promotion of these first two book projects is completely tested and placed it is my objective to use this system as my base platform for all further book launches. This would then include digital marketing blitz, book tours signing, printed sales distribution. Your book must be available for return to make the shelves. This requires Ingram and/or Baker Taylor distribution connection.

Resources for Reference the Websites

New York Times Best Seller List:

http://www.forbes.com/sites/jeffbercovici/2013/02/22/heres-how-you-buy-your-way-onto-the-new-york-times-bestsellers-list/

Social Engaged Publishing (pay after the published results process) There is much less profit for the author in this approach but the cost up front is significantly lower for those that are trying to bootstrap a book to market this might be a very good resource.

http://booktrope.com/booktrope-publishing/

Buying your way onto the Best Seller Lists is possible but pretty expensive. Here is one of the best firms in the business. Check them out here. http://www.resultsource.com/

This firm handles the best and brightest gurus and self made folks to make sure their book debuts are spectacular. They are a major source of fee-based success for those with the cash to see it through.

Folks I have found to be credible for your own Do-It-Yourself-Promotion campaigns and publishing resources are as follows;

Authoright: http://www.authoright.com/

Novel Publicity: http://www.novelpublicity.com/

Bookmasters:
http://www.bookmasters.com/marketing_netwidget_google.html?gclid=COeG-NTL5LkCFeqDQgodsVwAew

Vividi websites: http://www.vividcandi.com/agency-pricing/
(very expensive $5k+)

Webdesign Relief:
http://www.webdesignrelief.com/affordable-design-pricing/

Enovel Reviews: http://enovelreviews.com/

Bookbub: http://home.bookbub.com/advertise

Bookbaby: http://www.bookbaby.com/ebook-publishing/publish-on-baker-and-taylor

Writers Relief: http://www.writersrelief.com/

Writers submission services: http://writerssubmission.com/

Writers Digest:

http://www.writersdigest.com/writersresources

Book Blast: http://www.bookblast.com/

Book Daily: http://www.bookdaily.com/

Pump Up Your Promotions:

http://www.pumpupyourbook.com/book-blasts/

Kindle Nation: http://kindlenationdaily.com/

Ebookit: http://www.ebookit.com/index.php

ERelease/PRweb: http://www.ereleases.com/submit.html

Advanced Reader Copies

http://www.millcitypress.net/marketing/services/advance-reader-copy or http://www.infinitypublishing.com/additional-book-publishing-services/advance-reading-copies.html

Copyright Services:

http://www.bookwhirl.com/Services/AlaCarte/US-Copyright.php

LCCN: Library of Congress Control Number:

https://www.createspace.com/Services/LCCNAssignment.jsp

Independent Universal ISBN:

https://www.createspace.com/Products/Book/ISBNs.jsp

Editors:

Laurie Rosin- http://www.thebookeditor.com/

David Compton- http://www.authoredit.com/

Karen Charlton- http://www.fameltonwritingservices.com/

Cover Designers:

Erik Hollander- https://www.elance.com/s/erikhollander/

Jamie Zvirzdin- http://www.jamiezvirzdin.com/

Book illustrators:

http://www.illustrationweb.com/

Screen Play Productions:

I have found two very credible sources that I believe are fairly reasonable and that have good references.

Erik Mertz- http://erickmertzwriting.com/

Kathy Krantz- http://screenplayfactory.homestead.com/

You can also hire a service from the many book-publishing companies but the fees I have found are a bit higher and the service would probably be less exclusive in my own evaluation and opinion.

Ghost Writers: These services can be expensive but many folks need a good bit of help with organizing their story and getting it into readable format. This can be as simple as rewriting and working with you on a chapter-by chapter basis with direct input all along the way by the Author or a complete concept ghost written with very little input from the author. Of course the latter is fairly expensive and does not retain nearly as much of the author's creative voice, but all ranges are available based on your over-all budget. A top notch thriller ghost written will run approximately with author input from $5.00 per page to $30.00 per page or more generally, depending on the qualifications of the ghost writer.

https://www.elance.com/p/lpg/writing/ghostwriters?rid=1T
N5N&utm_source=google&utm_medium=cpc&utm_campaign=
C-Writing-Person-
Exact&utm_term=ghost%20writers&ad=28950852018&bmt=

e&adpos=1s1&gclid=CKKlrqrc5LkCFe1_QgodziUAZg

http://associationofghostwriters.org/

One of the Best I have found but he is very reclusive:

Joel Corenman- (do not contact him directly please ask for introduction) from me.

https://www.facebook.com/joel.corenman

http://www.amazon.com/McKinley-Summit-ebook/dp/B0058ZY1IY

http://www.imdb.com/name/nm1298802/

Literary Legal & Professional Representation:

At a minimum you will want to get your book an independent ISBN for each format it is published in. Plus I recommend a copyright and a copy sent to the Library of Congress as well. This gives you the broadest range of coverage.

http://www.wga.org/

https://www.awpwriter.org/

http://naiwe.com/

http://www.societyofauthors.org/

http://www.asja.org/

http://www.independent-authors.org/

http://www.rightsofwriters.com/2010/12/44-places-where-writers-and-other.html

http://www.kayemills.com/about.html

http://www.lennieliterary.com/

If you begin to deal with screenplay selling and/or traditional publishing make sure you have proper legal representation from an established attorney with background in such transactions.

Self-Publishers & Emerging Author Traditional Publishers:

Friesen Press-

http://welcome.friesenpress.com/s/usa?gclid=CPidr6DY5LkC FYU5QgodqlAA9w

This service seems to represent about the best of the self-publishing built in turn key promotional publishing houses. Their turnkey best service is $4995.00

CreateSpace Amazon-https://www.createspace.com/AboutUs.jsp

This is the best place for a new author that does not want to pay for a bunch of self-publishing services and/or wishes to purchase them ala carte. I have found their site and services to be flawless and work exceptionally well. They do have limitations such as one digital format (kindle) and no hardcover formats. They are owned by Amazon.

Xlibris- http://www2.xlibris.com/

They have a solid track record and good services albeit very slow customer service and pesky and annoying sales and marketing department that will hound you for new marketing services all the time. I have used a number of their services for marketing and found them to be not very cost-effective. They are quite pricey and have little accountability for feedback. They also pay quarterly and have an antiquated sales royalty system. Xlibris touts their ownership by Random House but it seems to be over stated.

Authorhouse- http://www.authorhouse.com/

They have a broad range of services all the way to book to film services. The services seem pricey similar to Xlibris but I believe their services at Authorhouse are more robust with a wider offering if that is your taste.

Baker Street Publishers- http://bakerstreetpublishing.com/

This group is very proficient at developing marketing and speaking platforms for authors that want to self-promote their services as a professional paid keynote or celebrity speaker. They do the soup to nuts approach on the talking points and speech.

Taylor Street Publishing- http://www.taylorstreetbooks.com/

A group that is a bit mysterious. You have to get recommended before they will allow you to submit a manuscript for consideration. Currently they have a few books that seem to be doing well. They are a small niche publisher... always a good starting point for new authors seeking to break into the book industry.

Cedar Fort Publishing- http://cedarfort.com/

A very friendly group that does consider new authors for submission, but they are very exclusive in who they actually represent. They are very helpful in providing contacts for editorial assistance and do allow you to resubmit once you have completed your edits.

Morris Press-

http://www.morrispublishing.com/who/intro.asp

They are a pay for production book publisher out of Nebraska that started in the cookbook industry and has evolved into the paid production book business. They can produce limited runs of your book for distribution to a central warehouse distribution center such as Baker Taylor and/or Ingram.

Literary Agent Lists:

The most important thing a new author must do is to become educated on the Query process and submission protocol used for submitting manuscripts for consideration to the traditional publishing world. I also believe you should use some Query letter publishing services to create the best first impression. These resources should give you a good over-all understanding of the process and resources so you do not make a bad impression in your search for literary representation if you decide to go that route. Patience is the greatest virtue in this type of endeavor.

http://aaronline.org/MAgents

http://www.agentquery.com/

http://www.sfwa.org/real/

http://www.writersdigest.com/editor-blogs/guide-to-literary-agents/literary-fiction-agents

http://www.mediabistro.com/galleycat/manuscript-wish-lists-on-twitter_b73317

http://www.querytracker.net/top-10-agents.php

Book Review Resources:

These are solid book review sources for getting the word out about your book to various reading circles. A difficult group to find without such referenced resources for your use. The amount you can spend and the individual value they can create for you and exposing your book can range greatly in price and outcomes. In the end, humans are very fickle and unpredictable creatures. The best reviews do not promise a good review but a fair one, and you need to accept that for what it is, or not pay for such services. Otherwise the cost of a fair and impartial review has been wasted.

http://yourfirstreview.com/?gclid=CPL2lMOx4LoCFZFxQgodl EgAvw

http://www.thekindlebookreview.net/get-reviewed/

http://onlinebookclub.org/

http://www.thereadingroom.com/home

http://www.bookreviewclub.com/about-us/

https://www.goodreads.com/book/show/13185469-the-next-america

http://www.theindieview.com/indie-reviewers/

http://www.compulsivereader.com/

http://www.booksneeze.com/

http://www.authorsden.com/

http://www.blueinkreview.com/

http://www.bookwire.com/

http://www.kirkusreviews.com/author-services/

https://www.forewordreviews.com/services/book-reviews/

http://www.hollywoodbookreviews.com/

http://www.pacificbookreview.com/

Example Template for the Twelve Step Hybrid Publishing Process

"The 18-month Publishing Book Plan"

You should look at your 12-step process as a campaign. Each of the areas of focus is divided into major categories. For example this campaign is post actual writing of your manuscript, which in itself is no easy feat. Steps one through four are part of the critical infrastructure phase. Steps five through nine are the marketing blitzkrieg or lighting attack on the industry for promotional purposes to seat your book in the social media, traditional media and gain readership. Step ten is the very critical mission or campaign review phase to determine what worked and what did not work and where was your money sell spent or not. Step eleven is

Step One:

Date Commenced: October 2013   Cost $580.00 and $275

Advanced Reader Copies $275 infinity Publishing or Lulu (9th Templar)

Synopsis of the book Famelton Writing services $580 plus another $145 in 2nd month.

Campaign with Bookdaily & Kindle Nation $147

Step Two

Date Commenced: Month: Cost: $449.95

Services & Cost: Writers Relief Query Letter Service (Ala Carte Plus)- $250.00 this generates 25 submissions targeted to your genre.

Writers Digest 2nd draft query letter review $39.95 (you should get their letter reviewed for a second opinion. Plus Famelton synopsis for $145, and excellent writers resource I have found and very reasonably priced for what you get.

Marketing- Kindle nation, Bookdaily, book blast- $347... this get's your direct exposure to the e-book readers in massive numbers.

11.   Facebook Covers – $40 (Author's Site)
12.   Facebook Insets – $20
13.   Twitter Backgrounds – $60
14.   Twitter Headers – $40

Date Commenced: **Step Three:**   Cost: $498.00

Marketing Campaign- Kindle Nation, Bookdaily, Ebookit- (TNA) - $493

Bookbaby Epublication $299.00 (includes formatting & distribution)

IPad Conversion $199.00 Bookbaby... ARC copies for 9th Templar

Date Commenced: **Step Four:**   Cost: $400.00

Author Bio by Novel Publicity- $50.00 (TNA)

E-book Discussion Guide for book clubs- $350.00 (TNA)

Date Commenced: **Step Five:**   Cost: $400.00

Book Trailer by Novel Publicity- $400.00 Package #1 (TNA)

Date Commenced: **Step Six:**   Cost $495.00

Website design and deployment- Webdesign Relief Open mike package with $400 in additions. Paid in second month. (Author Website)

Date Commenced: **Step Six (b)** Cost $400.00

SEO optimization

Blog incorporation

Google analytics

Social Media incorporation

Date Commenced: **Step Seven** Cost $399.00

Kindle Nation email blast (2 months) (9th Templar)

Date Commenced: **Step Eight** Cost $747.00

Bookdaily Email Blast (3 months) $147 (TNA)

Book Bub (social media promotion) cost $600 (TNA)

Date Commenced: **Step Nine** Cost $380.00

Ebookit (media press release $195 plus $195 for email promotion to 100 top media outlets. (TNA)

Date Commenced: **Step Nine (b)** Cost

$349.00

Kindle Nation SEO/FB promotion

Date Commenced: **Step Nine (c)** Cost

$259.00

Kindle Nation Silver Option

Date Commenced: **Step Nine (d)** Cost

$529.00

Kindle Thriller of the Week (9th Templar)

Date Commenced: **Step Nine (e)** Cost

$298.00

Kindle Nation Email blast (2 months) (9th Templar)

Date Commenced: **Step Ten** Total Cost
$5,497.00

Evaluation of the entire marketing campaign with sales production numbers laid in 30 and 60 days post campaign tool laid out in a twelve-month format. Once this is completed consider repeating the most successful formats for an additional six months.

Date Commenced: **Step Eleven:** Cost $3095.00

Authoright or Result Source media campaign

This campaign will depend upon the success of the original bootstrap campaign. If we reach sales of 2510 E-books we cover our original outlay. If sales exceed this to 3925 books we proceed to Authoright and use their service. Sales must exceed this number or we simply repeat steps one through ten again until we reach a 3925 benchmark per campaign.

If sales exceed 3925 by 10,000 copies then we proceed to the Result Source Best Seller, Web marketing and book tour campaign services. Once sales reach 50,000 copies we launch the book tour across the US. (They only work for traditionally published authors.)

Date Commenced: **Step Twelve:** (fiction book only)

Cost: $5,000

Once sales exceed 6,000 books we proceed to produce the Screenplay and position the book for movie right intellectual property sale with Kathy Krantz Screenplay Factory productions. Hire Erik Mertz for the additional solicitation publications another $2500.00 for the treatment. Total Cost this step $7500.00

Post Production Comments:

If you follow this template you have created the most cost-effective approach to building and branding yourself as a successful and highly profitable author on the global stage. Obviously you will be happy with my advice. This is the plan that I am using myself, so obviously I believe in it. I spent over four years learning and studying the best techniques that I felt were within reason of my being able to afford to pay as I go as a struggling and hard working writer/author/artist. I had to create a budget that allowed me to use my monthly discretionary money of what I decided I was willing to risk investing in myself. I based this on $500 per month as my bootstrap budget. This does not mean that you might be able to find less expensive approaches. I did self-promotion for the past 18 months on my own self-published platforms and managed to create approximately a $100 to $200 per month average sales production on all platforms. I found E-book and Audio books outperformed by printed books hands down. It was after this experiment that I decided to spend the next 18 months focused on those formats first before spending any more money and effort on the printed versions. This also preserved my ability to move my books to a traditional publisher if I successfully landed a good literary agent during the campaign. Good Luck

Prepublication Phase for Fiction Novel:

Every accomplished Author always has a book in the making so they are usually in the flux of writing their rough manuscript and/or getting it edited and reviewed by trusted and unbiased third party folks to improve it for eventual readership consumption in the market. I am no different. I try to have at least one book in edits all the time for eventual launch. I also try to be working on the idea and writing down my thoughts on my next manuscript. I keep an entire library of short story ideas I would like to work on in my lifetime. I try to keep one active all the time.

Here is my approach for the **9th Templar** Fiction book edits:

1.) Hire CreateSpace Evaluation Edit- $199

2.) Famelton Written book synopsis $145

3.) Final Edit Create Space comprehensive edit $2600

4.) Advanced Reader Galley Book production (50-100 copies) $275

5.) Final Developmental & Polish Edits $7500 (Only if windfall for consulting closes and funds)

6.) E-book format for advance digital sales only $399

7.) Copyright $79

8.) Unique ISBN $99

9.) Library of Congress Number $49

10.) Writers relief submission services $250

11.) Enovel reviews/Bookbub/kindle Nation/bookdaily/PrNew/Ebookit $2300 for full promotion campaign over 5 months

12.) Professional trailer with voice over $2200

13.) Final Cover $900

14.) Artwork $2000 sketches

15.) Book formatting and layout interior $1600

16.) E-book discussion guide for reader clubs $350

17.) Social media branding $160

18.) Authorit $3095 blast to media and news service

19.) Unique Website $800

20.) Reviews and promotion Smith Publicity $3497

Total Campaign Cost Evaluation = $29,077 = 10,422 E-books to Breakeven

Sunk cost breakeven evaluation- $27,900 = 10,000 books to breakeven

Combined Sales to Break even – 20,422 books / 50% ROI = 30,633/ 100% ROI = 40,844 book sales total. My total sunk cost = $56,977 Total Production Costs. *this book was edited heavily and I have included all my external costs.

Additional Services to Consider but not within the budget:

Amazon Optimization Service: Making Your Book's Amazon Page As Search Friendly And Appealing As Possible Your Amazon Optimization Consultant will:

15. work with you to create key words or "Tags," to increase search-ability,

16. direct numerous people on their team to your book with these key words to continue to drive up the search-ability of your book,

17. link your book to other best-selling books in your genre so that when a browser looks for a best-selling author in your category, they have a better chance of finding your

book,

18.   create an in-depth book description and author bio for Amazon's main book page, plus a separate author page augmented with links to your "assets" such as your book trailer, website, social media, and update ongoing press clippings, and

19.   provide "Search Inside" uploads, if needed.

The fee for the Amazon Optimization Service is $1,225 per book.

Amazon Top Reviewer ServiceTargeting Key Reviewers to Write and Upload Reviews to Your Amazon PageYour

Amazon reviewer consultant will present your e-book(s) to the top Amazon reviewers and encourage top reviewers in your genre to post reviews on your page. These reviewers have thousands of followers and a review from them drives traffic to your book page. A review from a top reviewer is not easy to get, but this team works with these influential group every day and presents your book in a timely and cost-effective manner.

The fee for the Amazon Top Reviewer Service is $1,925

per book. Please let me know if you're interested in further exploring one or both of the service options. If so, I'd love to introduce you to our Amazon services consultant. I believe the best choice for this campaign would be the Smith Publicity Group. I have been most impressed with their client feedback and their stylistic approach to these type campaigns.

Dina Barsky, Publicist and Sales Associatefor SMITH PUBLICITY, INC.(856) 489-8654 x319Dina@smithpublicity.com

Total cost of this service is $3,497

**Please remember that these prices and services are subject to change and cannot be depended upon as accurate at your own time of publication. You should always get current quotes for all vendor services and check current references prior to making a purchase.

Don Allen Holbrook

WHO ARE YOU AS AN AUTHOR?

CHAPTER 7

This chapter is very short on purpose. While the volume of written words may not be enormous the power of the questions posed in this short chapter merit considerable and very in-depth consideration by you personally. If you rush through this in an effort to complete what you see as an exercise to complete some ego outlet then you have missed the entire purpose of the chapter and probably this book's message.

If you have chosen the noble cause of writing to express your passion then it can be a very fulfilling personal experience and one that creates it's own rewards for us as author's that only other authors' can comprehend. It is a deeply satisfying outlet of a very emotional inner you. You are allowing your deepest secrets, observations and feelings to be exposed to the core at the very root of your actual existence if you are being honest and earnest in your endeavor of becoming an accomplished author. The pursuit of being an author in my opinion should not be primarily for notoriety, adoration of your peers and fans, fame and fortune, but rather a highly personal journey of you as a person at your very soul level. The best authors can move us to tears, anger, and romantic inclination, desire for adventure to see new places and a deep desire and yearning for more exposure to the story line. This makes authors highly special creatures amongst us humans. They can enlist a great range of emotion from others, so much so that we pay them to do so and for their continuation of their craft if they are masterful at it. Just like professional athletes, authors can become very famous and rich from the mastery of their craft.

It is also very similar to other exponential growth careers where you can go from nobody to star in a very short period of time, such as acting, performing artists, painters, etc. Once you are discovered if you are truly great, all of the accolades I mentioned before will surely be available to you, whether you sought them or not. Humans love to be entertained, especially in venues that we ourselves cannot normally do very well. Just consider sports, acting, singing, painting, and yes writing. All of these specializations come with great personal sacrifice of your privacy but with very lucrative financial rewards and stardom in many cases from our fans.

I believe it is for this purpose that you should undertake this short but highly personal exercise and answer the following questions for yourself. Write them down. Use them in your author biographies on your website, send them out in your press kits. It is the very reason that others have found your work special in my opinion. It communicates to our fans who we are, why we do what we do, and what we are doing it for? Who do we see as our audience and why?

What defines you as an author? Who do you think you are and how do you see yourself or how would you like to be seen by others?

"What would you say describes what your character and personal belief system are and what drives your passion as an author?"

Why did you choose to write and become an author?

"Think of this as an interview question from a media reporter, it

could very well be someday that this question becomes the basis for your sound byte if that interview does happen, and you definitely want this to sound polished, professional but also laced with personal moving passion."

As an author if you cannot make such statements most people will find it highly suspect that your writing would be much different. Contrary to popular belief, many authors are eloquent public speakers with great command of oratory skills. They are not all introverts that shy away from public exposure and the limelight. In fact, great authors at their heart are simply the storytellers of pre-written communications. Being an art is to be a great storyteller. Something that humans have treasured through out our existence.

Who do you see as your typical fan and why do you think they read your works?

"Again, this is a deep search into your own drive and passion to examine who you have observed that your writing seems to resonate with and why you believe it does so, or better yet, what others have exemplified to you for how your work positively impacts them."

If you keep these three simple questions present in your own mind, developed and honed into your author platform and make it part of your normal elevator pitch, it will create intrigue and interest in you and thus your work. It should be a very well thought out and heartfelt one page summary that you can refer to over and over again to reinforce the WHO YOU ARE, and the WHY YOU DO THIS and WHO DOES IT REACH questions that we ourselves need to understand and others will find interesting.

BUILDING YOUR AUTHOR PLATFORM

CHAPTER 8

I am going to keep this chapter short and sweet and refer to my previous chapters on business case and marketing development. Any author that has any real value has to develop their own style of a platform. Let's remember that an author needs to be fearless, write daily and exercise their opinion and collaborate with others normally to be successful.

Thus your Authors platform should reflect those values and make doing them easier and more organized for you to utilize. I believe in keeping this stuff simple and within a reasonable persons budget.

There are several major needs in this realm. You need to have outreach to potential collaborators and fans to develop a following. That is what a platform is all about.

Here is a list of normal questions a traditional publisher will ask you if you get to the stage where they actually have some interest in investing in YOU and YOUR book. The process of getting published usually requires that one of the genre editors takes your work to their own internal editorial board and they each discuss the pros and cons of taking you on as an author.

Here are the typical initial early stage questions: (now remember in this example, this is my own promotion using a hybrid approach for my non-fiction book as advocated in this book.) These questions were posed to me from real traditional publisher's editorial team.

1.) How many copies of your book have you sold since its release (please break this into hard copies and e-copies, if applicable)? What have your main sales avenues been?

2.) Have you written any other books? How well have they sold?

3.) Do you do any seminars, speaking engagements, etc. that may be an avenue for sales?

4.) How much traffic do you get on your website, blog, Twitter, Facebook, or other social media sites each month? Please give me any applicable URLs. If you don't currently maintain these things, would you be willing to start?

5.) Do you have any contacts in the media (think newspapers, TV, bloggers, magazines, etc.) or in the political sphere from whom you could secure endorsements, or who would be able to help you promote your book?

So as you can see from a publishers typical line of questioning they will ask of you... in addition, many of them will ask how many Twitter Followers you have? How many Facebook Friends you have? And how many LinkedIN and/or direct email contacts you have access to that have some knowledge of your personally and/or professionally?

Now you can see why the effort of building your platform is not only useful but very necessary.

My recommendation is that you immediately build your own presence on the following Social Media sites:

1.) Twitter- great for blasts of short pearls of info.

2.) Facebook- specific author's group

3.) LinkedIn-professional contacts.

4.) Google Contacts (circles)

5.) YouTube create your own Channel

6.) Amazon Author Central page

7.) Authors Den- readers site

8.) GoodReads- site for book reviews

9.) The Reading Room

10.) Net Galley

11.) Barnes & Noble Authors page

12.) WordPress- great blog site for authors

13.) Your personal Author Website (owned by you)

By creating a strong voice and presence in these areas it will spread the ease of finding you and the value of your platform to your potential publisher and yourself for sales.

It is very important to incorporate into your daily activities the pursuit and acquisition of everyone you meet into a digital format that can then be incorporated through invitation into your platform. Building a platform takes time and daily effort. I make it a habit to start by gathering everyone I meets email, and mobile phone number, then I search these platforms each day to determine if they have a presence. If they do I immediately send them a request to connect. I also invite them to my circles and my special pages that support my work. I would estimate that upwards of 90% respond and accept the connections. In less than two years I was able to build m Facebook contacts to over 2,500 and my LinkedIn contacts to over 3,300. That creates a potential sales platform of over 5800 contacts. Their own subject matter expertise and interests divide most of my LinkedIn contacts to me from my own perspective. I also have my own list of emails I have compiled from my own speaking and professional interactions. This list is over 16,000 folks in my own database. This type of contact power, where the author has had previous exposure to real people that can be documented and validated gives a publisher real significant foundational value to considering if the investment might be worth meriting. Without this type of support infrastructure it is much more difficult for an emerging author to become contracted for publication.

Now once you have these tools up and operational you should heavily consider getting help in making them all 100% very polished and professional. I believe paying for the polishing is much more beneficial than paying for someone to set them up for you in the first place. My basis for this statement is that most of us cannot afford to pay for the level of modifications that are normally necessary to keep these sites functioning at their highest usefulness and creating value for us. If you do not understand how to operate and use these sites yourself most of the time the process is far more costly than most of us can afford and usually this leads to a flat or dead site that has little if any value to the people connected to you and thus none to a publisher whether self or traditional.

The final value of your platform is in increasing your exposure and reach as an author. Search engine optimization SEO, is critical to building your power of being discovered. Search engines get smarter every day. Tags no longer fool them and key word blasts. They look for deep relevance to the key word through external linkages (think of them as exposures or views or page mentions) this traffic of external exposure and click through rates creates the internal credibility factor that now drives modern search engines.

This may sound overly simple but the best way to sell your book is to get it mentioned by lots of people in customer review comment boards, blogs etc. If you purposely send out request to your platform to request they give you a quick comment or review many of them will do so, even without having read your book. This increases your value in the search engine world exponentially as it ranks you placement based upon such mentions.

Today the smart author is constantly writing on their blog, requesting reviews and customer comments and feedback, because it drives value to their platform. Even if you are traditionally published you will need to incorporate all of my recommendations, so you might as well develop the right habits from the beginning.

Don Allen Holbrook

GETTING BOOK REVIEWS

CHAPTER 9

I wish I could tell you that all reviews are good reviews and all reviews are valuable, but I can't do so without tongue in cheek.

The most personally valuable reviews are those done without solicitation and coming from a genuine interest in our work of expression. Most of us as authors do generate a small amount of those from our close friends and our avid fans. But getting people to take the time to go to the various review sites that drive search engines and our sales is very difficult. As much as our family, friends and fans may love us, most are just too busy to take the time to make such efforts. But as an author we need these to be competitive so there has to be a major focus on getting what we need posted and not by our own hand directly.

Just as in the exercise of writing there are NO RULES or at least not many when it comes to promotion of our work for third party examples. If you are a die hard purist then you should probably just not read this chapter, well for that matter, this entire book is probably not up your ally. You are either exceptionally lucky if you have gotten published traditionally and/or if you are self-published probably not making very much money from your book sales. That is the sad reality for those who foolishly hold onto outdated principles that are not practiced in the mainstream by current authors. In simple fact, you either compete and keep up or get left behind in this modern society of instant information, and instant gratification.

For those of you that want to generate sales and real interest in your books then you should read on and follow this model carefully if you desire very positive results.

Let's divide the Types of Reviews into three categories:

1.) Friends, Fans and Family that give actual self-created reviews. These are genuine pearls of pride for any author, but even a New York Times best selling author may have a fairly short list of this type. Let's say less than a thousand. A fairly good benchmark for an Indie Self-Published author might be 10 to 20 such client or customer reviews. Even 10 are probably more than most in that publishing realm.

2.) Paid Professional Reviews (unbiased) these type reviews re from the original review houses out there. They are normally considered to be Kirkus Review, Foreword Clarion, Your First Book Review, Kindle Book Reviews, Pacific Book Reviews, BlueInk Book Reviews and Hollywood Book Reviews... and there are several others that charge for unbiased reviews. The fees can average $150 to $450 for such reviews. Each of these services should provide their reviews to be placed on all the major book sellers websites under your product, at least the big ones, such as Amazon, Barnes & Noble and the list of major independent book sellers. That is what they are paid for to get your review spread out to all the major sites. This does increase your exposure and thus search engine value. There are many unpaid independent reviewers that will give you a review if you post your work and they are interested in your genre and subject matter explanation. These are more time consuming to create and find, but some effort should be legitimately placed into the pursuit of these type reviews as well.

3.) Paid Bulk Reviews and BOOK CLUBS can be a tricky business. There are only a few that I have found to be credible and these types of reviews can also be expensive. They know the value of leveraging the search engines on the book sites and you do pay for that effort. This can be broken down further by sorting them by type... bulk versus book club orientation. I prefer the book club orientation. I recommend in my book campaign that authors invest in a book club media kit, and FAQ guide for book clubs that choose to read your book and author bio, for this exact purpose. These services can build readers and reviews with the circle of avid book readers in book clubs around the world. They may be a quiet bunch but almost every city and town has book clubs. They make great launch party and reader circle events for authors that are traveling and build a vibrant and viral fan base. Still the book club circle needs constant cultivation and promotion to get your book on their radar. You can also pay for this service. Some of the big ones are as follows; Booksneeze, The Book Review Club, Online Book Club, The Compulsive Readers Club, and a many others. This work can pay off in spades over time.

Another service you can utilize is a paid book blast blogger focus where a service promotes your book to many blogger sites over a campaign period. Some of these services also combine social media parties for readers where they promote you and give away some type of prize for those that attend the party. The incentives get visibility for your book. I have found one very credible source for this is PUMP UP YOUR BOOK. Dorothy Thompson runs this service out of Virginia. She does excellent hands on job of making it polished and professional. Here is my own book example;

http://www.pumpupyourbook.com/2013/11/07/pump-up-your-book-presents-the-next-america-book-blast-win-25-amazon-gift-card/

DEALING WITH SUCCESS OR REJECTION

CHAPTER 10

Now that you have taken the time to consider writing your first book, it is time to reflect upon your own desired outcomes and how you will personally deal with any number of possible scenarios. Consider this when you choose to pick up the pen or a better example today is put finger to keyboard, how will I feel if I do not meet my own expectations? Those of us that write, at least the vast majority, know the lonely feeling of a failed book campaign, a favorite book that just did not reach the mark of what we felt it deserved, rejection letters from literary agents, and/or the loss of financial investment when we put forth our best and most noble effort to succeed. Before you choose this profession you need to make sure your ego can withstand a torrent of rejections, critical reviews that do not get your message or disagree with you in a toxic and blusterous manner. You may have to endure bloggers that assail you and public reticule and/or friendships that sour over your expression. You may not have to endure them, but in this modern age of viral social media where transparency is none existent getting attacked for your work is very possible and quite plausible.

It is my own opinion that you should start with the worst-case scenario and work backwards from there. How will you deal with all of this negative exposure, public ridicule, online posts by vile unknown anonymous bloggers and reviewers who spew and attack you for your efforts? If you cannot comprehend this type of situation and you are not a realist that you will be critiqued at every aspect of your life and work, then you are not in the modern age of social media, the Internet and the new cyberspace antics that are so prevalent today at our instant exposure in our pockets, at work and at home. Society is mobile, armed with information and opinions and very capable of creating a juggernaut or tidal wave of negative media exposure for you and YOUR FAMILY.

Now, if you can prepare yourself for that possibility and can accept the fate of exposure to the masses then you should proceed in your endeavor.

Now the final question can be pondered. What does success look like to you? How would you define if you have become a successful author? This does not necessarily mean fame and fortune it should be highly personal. If you don't know what success looks like then how will you ever find satisfaction from the rewards of exposing your work?

For many of us, this equation plays out in dribs and drabs. Perhaps success initially is the achievement of just completing the work you feel so inclined to create and expose the world to at your own personal expense emotionally, professionally, and financially.

The next level is usually, how can I get heard by more people? Not necessarily how can I make more money or make enough money to make a living at this or even repay my investment into my efforts, but rather how can I get my work noticed and as such get satisfaction of feeling some additional accomplishment? This is when the real gut check ha to happen. Being an author or at least a successful one requires that you develop a business mindset. You must begin to develop your list of pros and cons to market penetration. What is your financial ability to engage and build your market? How much can you afford to spend becomes the question. Remember this is a business now and you must run it efficiently if you want it to eventually at least become self-sufficient. My secondary goal in this area was how could I create enough sales to repay my actual hard money costs I have spent to build, publish and distribute my books? I used this approach in my chapter on the business case. I had to attack the question with hard data and measurable outcomes over a specific time period. The answer is unique for each of us.

I have gotten great pleasure from helping a few of my friends follow their passions to write a book. The observation of personal pride and satisfaction they have each received made my time investment worth the effort. I do remember the advice I gave one of my closest friends in the world. He knows who he is, so I will not name him here. He called with an idea of a sure fired opportunity to invest in some business scheme. I was knee deep in my own investment in my book at the time, but I felt my friend-deserved support for his initiative. I remember telling him, "Why not actually spend far less money and have a win-win no matter what from your investment?" He was puzzled. He had told me he had always wanted to write a unique story about his family history, he felt it was very unique. I told him, then spend some time and money and write the story. No matter what happens your outcome will be something you highly value and the money will be spent on something that you will treasure for a lifetime. In other words, it was a failsafe investment.

I think this same philosophy applies to each of us and thus you should look at your financial investment as something that will pay dividends and create a legacy that can go far beyond your own time here on earth. Great authors are virtually immortalized and held in our thoughts and feelings for centuries. There is no promise of fame and fortune in this life, but it also can come after you have passed. Nonetheless, the pride of having been an author is something your family, friends and future generations will come to cherish through out your life and possibly beyond.

This is the essence of what being an author is all about. I believe it is something that can give you immense pride and satisfaction. I can make no promises of fame, fortune or even adoration, but I can tell you I find very few examples of authors who regret having become part of this noble and elite aristocracy of special people who record, thoughts, opinions and tell stories that are part of the very fabric of humanity.

I wish all of you the greatest success and the highest level of personal satisfaction from your endeavor into this special world of being an author. I believe you will never regret your investment of time, money and passion into this very special craft and artistic form of expression.

- God Bless You All... Happy Endings!

Don Allen Holbrook

ABOUT THE AUTHOR

Don Allen Holbrook lives in Las Vegas, Nevada with his wife and their two boys. He advocates that all of us individually should take responsibility to be accountable for the change we desire in our country, our own lives and our communities. The hope for our children and their own future generations is our responsibility to sustain.

He has lived a fast paced and globetrotting lifestyle for much of his business career. He enjoys writing because it allows him to express his thoughts and develop his inner voice on his own beliefs and follow his passion for his own life and that of his family while also advocating for progress within our own country in particular in the elected officials that represent us and their own lack of fiscal responsibility to our country. He believes the tax code needs drastic reform and overhauling but does not believe this means we should move away from capitalism.

He writes to create outlets for his passion of historical fiction set in modern day circumstances, action adventure thrillers with some type of conspiracy theory is his favorite genre. He often says they are the mysteries and stories we all wish would be told. Holbrook believes everyone has a great book in them and thus he thinks getting more of us started to write our own feelings, passions and thoughts is a worthy course for many folks.

The Sovereign Military Order of the Temple of Jerusalem, the Knights Templar Order, knighted Holbrook in 2010 at the USMA West Point. He continues to love to travel and write. He is an accomplished international keynote motivational speaker. He was given the honor of being named a Fellow Member of his International Economic Development Council in 2008.

He has spent over 23 years as an economic development expert consultant, speaker and author on the use of incentives and local business development policies to create jobs and attract capital investment to locales especially with the new pressures of the global economy and in the aftermath of the global financial crisis.